A Newbies Guide to the Microsoft Surface Tablet:

Everything You Need to Know About the Surface and Windows RT

Minute Help Guides

www.minutehelp.com

Table of Contents

Introduction

Since the introduction of the iPad in 2010, the entire world has gone tablet crazy. While Apple pretty much created the mainstream market for these devices, Microsoft actually got there first—hybrid tablet/laptops running Windows have existed since the 90s. Unlike Apple, Microsoft doesn't generally produce their own hardware; they prefer to let dozens of manufacturers fight over standards and pricing.

In fact, the Surface RT is the first computer Microsoft has *ever* made. When they decide to enter a market – like the home console space with the Xbox and the massively successful Xbox 360 – you can rest assured that they have something new to offer consumers. As you'll learn over the following pages, the Microsoft Surface Tablet is definitely something new. It's a pretty amazing device that takes everything you love about your tablet and laptop computer and somehow manages to improve on both concepts.

The Surface RT is one part of a larger reinvention of Microsoft's core product, the Windows operating system. Windows 8, a special version of which powers the new Surface Tablet, is the most significant update that Windows has ever seen. There's a little bit of a learning curve, but we're confident that by the time you finish reading this guide, you'll be singing the praises of this unique device to anyone who'll listen.

Ready? Let's jump right in!

Part One: Getting Started

What's in the Box (and what's not)

If you've bought any new tech gadget in the last few years, you've surely noticed that companies don't generally include every little thing you might need to get started anymore. Gone are the days of the all-inclusive box, and the Surface Tablet is no exception. What you'll get depends largely on what configuration you've ordered, and there are a few of them, each at a different price point:

- Surface RT -32gb ($499)
- Surface RT -32gb w/ touch cover ($599)
- Surface RT -64gb w/ touch cover ($699)

Microsoft also sells their 'Touch' and 'Type' covers separately, both for around $120. We'll discuss that in a moment.

As you can see, the Surface Tablet by itself is priced on par with other premium tablets like Apple's iPad or Samsung's Galaxy Tab 10.1. While the device seemingly has double the storage of the comparably priced versions of these tablets, the Windows RT operating system and other related files will take up a majority of that extra space, leaving you with about 18 GB of actual free space for your apps and personal files. The real difference is in the (optional) covers – this is where the Surface RT really blows away the competition.

Covers - While a lot of tablets have keyboard add-ons, not one of them has such an elegant, essential solution. The 'Touch' and the 'Type' covers are an engineering marvel. Microsoft has managed to fit an entire full-size keyboard into a razor-thin, magnetically attached protective cover:

While both the 'Touch' and 'Type' covers both include a laptop-like track pad, only the 'Type' cover utilizes actual keys. The 'Touch' cover just has a layout of the keys, with no actual moving parts. Neither of them require any power at all, they just connect to the bottom of your Surface tablet with a satisfying click and come to life.

> *It sounds strange (and nobody would blame you for being skeptical), but after a couple hours of practice, we were 'Touch' typing just as fast as we generally do on our trusty laptop keyboard. In fact, every word of this guide was written using a Surface RT with a 'Touch' cover.*

Since the Surface RT is designed to be a practical productivity tool, we highly recommend buying either one of these covers. If you decide against it, you're really only getting half of the Surface RT experience.

HDMI Cables - Once you open the box, you'll notice that there isn't much inside: you'll see the Surface tablet itself, a power cable (which connects magnetically, just like the cover), and a small white user guide. That's it. In fact, the user guide is really just warranty and electrical warnings in 3 languages.

As we'll discuss in the next section, the Surface RT comes with two ports: one USB and one Micro-HDMI. There are, as we've just seen, no cables to connect these ports to anything. If you're ever planning to hook up your Surface to a television set (we'll show you some cool things like this a little later), you're going to have to pick up an HDMI cable. Microsoft, like everyone else, seems to have jacked up the prices on these cables on their website, hoping to make a little extra cash from people who don't know any better:

These two cables are the same size, with the *exact same* connectors. They perform identically. The one on the left, priced at $39.99, is from Microsoft's official Surface Store. The one on the right, costing $5.76, is from noted (and reputable) cable supplier Monoprice.com. We're not accusing anyone of anything here—maybe that exorbitant price is a typo – but until they fix their mistake, go ahead and pick up a cable from Monoprice.com, Amazon, or eBay. Just search for Micro HDMI cable.

Headphones - Like most tablet devices, the Surface RT doesn't include headphones. We're not entirely sure why companies always seem to leave this out –headphones are generally included in just about every smart phone, so why not tablets?

While the Surface RT has a headphone jack, allowing you to use just about any set of headphones you already have, the device also has Bluetooth, which means you can pair it up with any Bluetooth headset you like. This can come in really handy for people who do a lot of video chatting via Skype.

That's about it for essential accessories. Beyond these three items, Microsoft has included everything you need to get the most out of your Surface RT.

Now let's dig a little deeper into the device itself.

Getting to Know the Surface Hardware

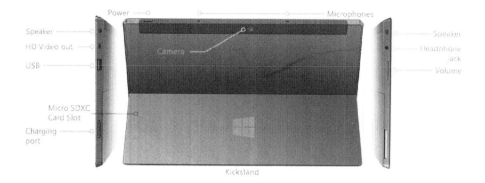

The Surface RT is an elegant piece of machinery – it's got a lot more going on under the hood than almost every other tablet in the marketplace. As you can see in the diagram above, Microsoft has included a few handy extras that users of other tablet devices have been clamoring for. The USB port, for instance, is an easy way to transfer files to and from the Surface (more on that later), but it's also a pragmatic way to future-proof it – third party companies will surely be making a bunch of Surface-specific accessories that use this USB port.

As it stands now, there are reportedly 420 million peripherals already in the marketplace that will work just fine with the Surface RT—things that you probably already own, like printers, USB game controllers, mice, and webcams. That's the advantage with using a Windows-based tablet: it's been the dominant computing platform for around two decades. Just head to **www.microsoft.com/compatibility** to check if your current devices (or one you're thinking about picking up) pass the compatibility test.

One of the most talked about features of your new Surface RT is undoubtedly the kickstand. It's a thin, yet *incredibly* strong built-in stand for your device. At 22 degrees when opened, it's pretty much the perfect angle for watching videos on the couch, or typing (with one of the covers) on a desk. Weirdly, Microsoft has hidden one of its least advertised features right behind the kickstand, and you might've gone months without noticing if we didn't bring it up: the MicroSD card slot. While your Surface came with either 32 GB or 64 GB of storage, this handy little slot (located on the left side, right above the charging port) will allow you to expand it by up to 128 GB. Check your local computer store for MicroSD card prices.

Beyond the kickstand, the extra ports, and the MicroSD slot, your Surface RT comes with the usual assortment of tablet goodies: stereo speakers, a headphone jack, rear and front-facing cameras, a power button, and volume buttons. It's also got the standard multi-touch screen, but—in another twist to separate it from the pack – it's a true 16:9 display, while most tablets (iPad included) use a 4:3 aspect ratio. It might not seem like a big deal, but if you're the type of person who watches a lot of movies on your mobile device, you'll be pleased to see that video takes up the entire screen here; no more of those annoying black bars on the top and bottom of the screen.

Making the display 16:9 has elongated the screen pretty significantly, so if you're used to holding other tablets in portrait mode, it might take some getting used to.

Now that we're a little more familiar with the Surface RT, let's begin setting up the device.

Powering on/ Initial Setup

Microsoft has made setting up the Surface as pain-free as possible. Much like the installation of desktop Windows, the setup mostly consists of a few questions and a whole lot of waiting for the device to do its thing. To get started, just press the power button on the top right of the device.

Once you've done that, you'll be presented with the language selection screen. Choose your language carefully, as the rest of the setup will continue in the language you've chosen. If your mastery of French isn't above a 3rd grade level, you're going to wish you'd stuck with English.

Once you've selected your language, you'll be presented with the 'License Terms' page. Make sure to read through the entire boring thing *at least* twice before tapping the 'I Accept' button.

Once you've done that, you'll be taken to the 'Personalize' page:

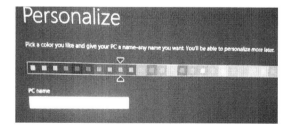

Here, you can slide your finger right or left to change the background, foreground, and text colors in pre-designed (non-clashing) ways. You'll also name your computer just like you would a Windows desktop. Don't worry too much about these choices; they're incredibly easy to change later on, with even more customization options.

Next, you'll be asked to connect to your wireless network. Just find your network in the list, highlight it by tapping on it (or clicking if you've connected a keyboard cover already), and tap connect. If your network is password-protected, you'll be prompted to enter your password. If you've connected a keyboard, just type it in – if not, an on-screen keyboard will automatically come up, allowing you to enter it that way.

Once that's done, you'll be given the option of turning on file sharing with all of the devices on your home network. Go ahead and tap 'yes', unless you're (for some reason) doing this initial setup at your local Starbucks or any other public Wi-Fi hotspot.

Once that's finished, you'll be presented with the express settings menu. Here, you'll be given a choice (just like in desktop Windows) of whether you'd like to go through all the possible settings, or let Microsoft choose the most common settings for you. Choosing express settings will skip the next few screens—and save you a couple of minutes—but it's worth it to go through them, if only to double check.

For this guide, we're going to assume that you've chosen 'customize' instead of 'express settings.' Feel free to skip ahead a little bit if this stuff doesn't apply to you.

The first batch of settings are basically Internet safety measures. Turning on SmartScreen will double check that any file you attempt to download or transfer to your Surface RT is free of viruses or malware.

The same holds true for the Internet Explorer SmartScreen filter – it will check a site's URL against a list of known bad ones, which can help eliminate the risk of popular phishing attacks.

The 'Do Not Track' feature will block websites from installing tracking cookies on your Surface RT. This one is more of a tinfoil hat, conspiracy item – some websites have legitimate reasons to track your location. Google, for example, uses cookies to track your whereabouts if your device isn't GPS-enabled, which applies to the Surface tablet. Leave it enabled if it's important to you.

The next settings menu entry is all about your Surface's interaction with Microsoft. The company uses tracking data themselves to help improve customer experiences. Again, if you're against this type of thing, don't enable anything on this menu. Microsoft doesn't mean any harm with this stuff, but they've still left the defaults in the 'off' position, just to make sure you don't accidentally join something you don't want to:

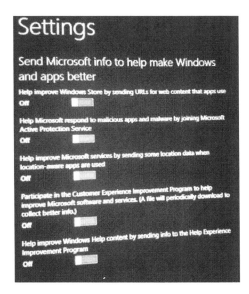

If you're sensing a pattern here, you'll be proven right by this next settings menu. This one is all about consumer privacy too. From here, you can decide whether downloaded apps can have access to your name and account picture. There's no reason why that should be a problem, but, again, if it makes you uncomfortable, Microsoft will let you opt out:

Once we're through navigating all of this privacy stuff, we're almost ready to complete the setup. The next screen will allow you to change your country, language, and keyboard input.

Once that's done, you'll be asked to 'sign in' to your Surface. If you've previously signed up for a Microsoft account, you'll already have the information you need here. Your Xbox Live email address or any address you've previously used to purchase anything from Microsoft will do.

If you don't have one, just type in your primary email address and choose a password. If you'd rather sign up for a new email address specifically for your Surface tablet, Microsoft has made that an easy task – just tap the 'sign up for a new email address' link near the bottom of the screen. For obvious reasons, you won't be able to create a new Gmail or Yahoo! Account – you'll have to make do with @live.com or @hotmail.com, both free email hosts managed by Microsoft.

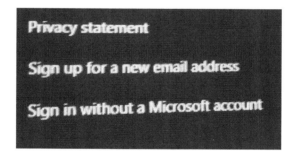

Once you've got the email situation squared away, the device itself will take care of the rest of the setup. You'll spend a few quality moments with this color-changing screen before you're thrust into the exciting world of Surface RT:

The Start Screen and Gestures

Now that you've completed the initial setup, you'll be brought into the system itself. While the interface was previously called 'Metro', Microsoft's new way of displaying your content and applications is now officially called the 'Start' screen. Versions of this layout appear on all of Microsoft's products this year: Windows 8, Xbox 360, and Windows RT, which is the operating system the Surface RT uses. For experienced Windows users, it's definitely a shock-to-the-system type of change:

Each one of those 'Live Tiles' that you see can be rearranged and resized. They will often contain real-time updates, as you can see from the 'Weather' tile towards the bottom of the picture.

At the bottom of your screen, there is a touch-sensitive button with the familiar Windows logo. Tap it to return to the Start screen at any time.

There are a bunch of finger gestures you'll have to become familiar with to take full advantage of this interface, but don't worry – you'll have it down in a few minutes, and it'll seem like the most obvious stuff in the world in less than an hour:

Tapping – this should be familiar to anyone who has ever used a touch screen device of any sort. To open a program, or select an option, just tap in the space where the program/option resides. For instance, tapping the 'Weather' tile we just discussed will open the 'Weather' app:

Tap and Hold – this will bring up options for whatever you're doing. This functionality is generally reserved for apps (like Office RT) as opposed to the Start screen.

Left-Right Swipe – swiping from the middle of the screen in either direction will scroll through the screen. The Start screen can actually be made up of several different screens, each with completely unique content. Swiping is the quickest way to find your way around.

Pinching and Zooming – using your thumb and index finger to make a pinching or stretching motion will allow you to zoom in or out of an object. This is incredibly useful for manipulating folders and pictures. For example, pinching to zoom out of the Start screen will bring up an overview of every tile on every Start screen.

Rotate Left or Right – Sort of like pinching, rotating your thumb and index finger will rotate the selected object right or left. Mainly used for games and for manipulating photos.

Quick Swipe – Selecting a tile and quickly swiping in a downward motion will bring up a context menu for that tile:

From here, you can remove the tile from the start screen (unpin from start), remove the application from the device (uninstall), make the tile larger or smaller, and stop the tile from displaying real-time information (turn live tile off). This last one can come in *very* handy. For example, you might want to turn off the live tile for email If you receive a lot of sensitive communications that you don't want displayed right on your Start screen.

The next four gestures are critical to working with Windows RT. They all involve swiping in from one edge of the screen.

Swiping in From the Right Edge – Swiping in from the right edge within any app, document, or Start screen will bring up what's called the Charms menu, which we'll discuss in detail a little later:

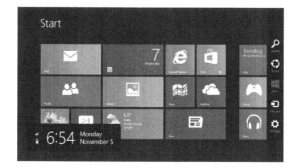

As you can see, in addition to the Charms menu on the right hand side, this action also brings up the date, time, Wi-Fi status, and battery life.

Swiping in From the Top or Bottom – This action will bring up the 'all apps' menu:

Swiping in From the Left – swiping in from the left will take you to the last open program on the device. Repeating this will switch from app to app in reverse order. If no apps are open, this action won't do anything at all. Doing this while using an app can do one of two things: switch to the previous app, or (if you drag the new app to the halfway point on the screen) split the screen into two apps that you can then use simultaneously.

Quick Swipe in From the Left to Right, Then Back – this one is a little bit tricky. If you swipe in from the left as if you're going to switch apps, then swipe left again without lifting your finger, you'll bring up the task switcher, which is a visual representation of all of your open apps:

Just like with the app switching gesture, if you have no open apps, this one won't function. It also won't function if you have only *one* open app.

That's pretty much it for touch gestures. All of these can be replicated using the track pad on your Surface Cover/keyboard. Use the left side as if it's a finger and you should be good to go. There is also a handy key on the keyboard that will take you directly to the Start screen. Look for it in the bottom left half of the keyboard, right around where you'd find the Start key on a traditional Windows keyboard.

Now that you've learned all about gestures and navigating your way around, let's take a deeper look at The Surface tablet.

Part Two: Using the Surface

The Charms Bar

If you've ever used an Android or Apple tablet, you may have already noticed something troubling: there's very little uniformity. There is no universal way to search for things within an app, and there's certainly no universal way to adjust settings. With the Surface RT, Microsoft has endeavored to fix this problem. Their incredibly elegant solution is called the Charms Bar.

We've already discussed how to swipe in from the right to bring up the Charms Bar, but what exactly does it do? Well, pretty much everything.

Search - This icon represents search. Tapping here will allow you to look for pretty much everything, beginning with the application you're currently in, but spreading (via a clever menu system) to everywhere else on the device:

Share – This icon will allow you to share any of the selected content currently being displayed, including pictures, news stories, weather—you name it. If there is nothing sharable onscreen, tapping the icon will tell you so:

There's nothing to share right now.

Start- this icon is just a toggle for the Start Screen. It functions in exactly the same way as the touch-sensitive button at the bottom of your device.

Devices – Tapping here will allow you to send (some) files and documents to devices you've previously paired with the device. Mostly used for printing and sending videos to enabled televisions.

Settings – Probably the most important function of the Charms Bar, this area is home to all of the settings for the application you're currently using. You can also access common device options and more advanced system-wide settings from here.

We'll get into the more advanced 'PC' settings a little later in this guide, but for most cases, the six icons toward the bottom are all you'll need:

Wi-Fi – accesses the Wi-Fi menu, allowing you to connect, disconnect, and search for available networks.

Volume – Controls the system-wide volume. Changing this setting will change the volume across the entire device. There are, however, task-specific controls located in the advanced settings menu, which we'll discuss a little later.

Screen – controls the screen brightness. Lowering the brightness can have a powerful effect on the battery life of your Surface.

Notifications – tapping this setting will hide all of your notifications (emails, breaking news, etc) for a specified period of time. It's incredibly useful when you're doing something that you'd prefer not be interrupted, like editing a document or watching a video.

Power – from here, you can shut down, restart, or put the system to sleep – just like with a traditional Windows PC. If there are updates to install, there will be an additional option here labeled 'Update and Restart.'

Keyboard – this area controls the on-screen keyboard function, allowing you to select an alternate pop-up keyboard. You can also bring up the handwriting recognition keyboard from here, which is kind of neat, though functionally useless.

That's pretty much it for 'Charm' school. Let's dig a little deeper now and go over all the applications that come pre-installed with your Surface RT.

Pre-Loaded Apps

As you've probably noticed already, your Surface tablet comes with a bunch of pre-installed applications. These are, more or less, the 'best of the best' applications, most of them made by Microsoft – a lot of them specifically for this device. Before you spend any time downloading apps, let's check out a few of the things your Surface can do right out of the box.

Mail – The ability to check (and write) emails is essential for any mobile device. This app keeps all the email from all your accounts in one convenient place. To get started, just tap the mail icon on the Start screen.

Before anything else, you'll be asked whether or not you'd like the mail app to run in the background. It's up to you, but allowing this will make sure that you know about it the *instant* you receive new mail, which is kind of the point of email in the first place, isn't it? Either way, once you've dealt with that, you'll be presented with a mostly blank, white screen. In the left hand corner, you'll see several options to add various email accounts. From here, you can configure accounts from AOL, Gmail, Yahoo!, Hotmail, Live.com, MSN, Outlook (including Exchange servers and Office 365), and even your own personal email accounts from custom domains, which is listed as 'Other' in the Charm Bar settings.

For this example, we added one of our Gmail accounts by tapping Gmail, then typing in our @Gmail address and the password. Within seconds, our mail was synced up with the device, allowing us to interact with our email in a totally intuitive way. It's a three pane system, with folders on the left, a list of emails in the middle, and the current email on the right:

Notice the three circles in the upper right hand corner. The trash can located on the far right will delete the current email. The letter with the arrow will bring up the reply options. The plus sign will bring up the new mail composition window:

Enter your recipient(s) in the left hand column and then add your subject on the top. Write your email and tap the letter (with wings) to send it. To exit, tap the x, which will allow you to delete the email or save it as a draft for later.

A quick swipe from either the right or left on an unread email will bring up set of options along the bottom of the screen:

From here, you can move an email into another folder or mark it as read/unread. Selecting multiple emails to do these things with is as simple as swiping left/right on as many emails as you like.

People – Before you go looking for apps like Facebook, Twitter, LinkedIn, or Messenger in the App Store, you might want to check out People first. This app collects all of the data from those and collates it all together into a magazine-style interface:

These screen shots are meant to give you an idea of how the People app functions. Names and photos will not be redacted in your People App.

In this example, we connected two of our social media accounts (Twitter and Facebook) by swiping in from the right to activate the Charms Bar and then tapping 'Add Account.'

The example above is the main screen of the People app. From here, you can see your notifications directly below your picture. This will tell you all about your unseen Facebook likes, comments, and/or messages, as well as Twitter Re-tweets, direct messages, and mentions. Tapping on any of your contact names will allow you to message that person using whatever apps they are also connected to. You can also view a person-specific newsfeed from here.

Tapping 'What's New' on the bottom will bring you to the unified news feed, allowing you to browse all of your friends' posts and Tweets, view comments, and add comments of your own:

Swiping up from the bottom (or down from the top) will bring up an options menu on the bottom of your screen:

Tapping Home will bring you back to the main People screen. Tapping Refresh will refresh your newsfeeds. Tapping Filter will bring up a dialog that will allow you to choose which feed you'd like to see, instead of the standard mix of everything. Tapping New Post will allow you to make a new post to whichever social media account you choose.

News – The News app is one of the best news aggregators we've ever seen on a tablet device. Even without customization, this app delivers constantly updated, real-time news from the best, most reliable sources.

To get started, just tap the News tile and wait for it to load. It should only take 20-30 seconds, and this will be the only time you'll have to wait. As you can see, the News app typically starts with a 'Top Story' collected from the Bing search engine:

Tapping the story will allow you to read it, while tapping the info button in the bottom right corner will bring up a short summary of it. Swiping to the left will show more news stories in several different categories. To dig deeper and show only stories within a category, just tap the news category on the top.

If that was all there is to this app, it'd be an awesome news reader. It's not: you can also read news from hundreds of specific magazines, newspapers, and websites. Just swipe up from the bottom (or down from the top) to bring up the news options:

Tapping Sources will bring up a massive list of news sites in every conceivable category. As an example, we pulled up technology and were greeted with this:

Tapping any one of those icons will bring you to a magazine style interface showing all of that site's recent stories. You can do this with every site within every category. There is a mind-boggling amount of news at your fingertips here.

As if that's not enough, you can also create your own customized news feed using any combination of keywords. To do this, just tap the My News icon. Swiping to the left will bring up the 'Add Sources' menu:

We decided to add the generic term 'Sports' to our feed, which immediately added a sports section to our news feed. You can do the same with practically any word or phrase you can think of. For example, if you're a tech news junkie, you might want to add Microsoft, Apple, or Google to your news feed. Doing this will show you any and all stories related to these companies. Pretty cool, huh?

Internet Explorer – Web browsing is another important feature of any tablet, and Microsoft certainly didn't skimp on that. There are actually two versions of Internet Explorer bundled with your Surface – a tablet optimized version accessible from the Start screen, and a more full-featured version accessible from the Desktop (more on that one later).

Many people are not fans of Microsoft's web browsing experience. A lot of people prefer Firefox, Safari, or Chrome, and consider IE to be a messy, inelegant throwback to the 90s web browsing experience. There used to be some truth to that, but the Surface RT version(s) are an absolute dream to work with: it's a fast, responsive, and intuitive experience.

To get started, just tap the Internet Explorer tile on your Start screen. You'll immediately be presented with the touch-optimized MSN for Windows 8 site. You'll also notice that the address bar is placed along the bottom, a departure from most other web browsers:

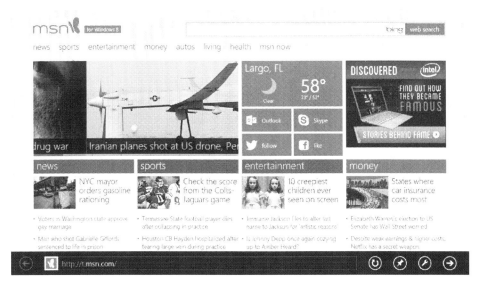

From here, you can type any URL into the address bar and tap Go. Alternately, you can search Bing by either tapping in the search field on the home screen or swiping in from the left to bring up the Charms Bar.

To open a new webpage without removing the current one, just swipe in from the top to bring up tab view:

You'll notice two icons on the right hand side. The plus icon will open a new tab. The bottom icon will allow you to open a new inPrivate tab (Microsoft's version of incognito browsing) or close all open tabs.

Along the bottom of the screen, to the right of the URL bar, you'll notice 4 more icons:

The circular arrow will re-load the current page. The straight arrow will move forward one page – assuming there's a page to move forward to. The wrench will bring up the 'find on page' dialog, and also allow you to view the current website on the desktop version of Internet Explorer (which we'll discuss a little later in this guide). If the webpage you're currently browsing has a Surface App related to it, you'll also be able to directly download it by tapping here.

The middle icon, the pushpin, is probably the most important. Tapping here will allow you to add the current website to a list of favorites. From here, you can also pin any webpage to the Start screen for instant access. As an example, we tapped Pin to Start while browsing the popular music website pitchfork.com, which brought up this box:

As you can see, the text is fully editable, which can come in handy. For example, if you want to create a shortcut to your bank's website, you can edit the text to simply say 'Banking' instead of Wells Fargo or Citibank. We decided against editing it, tapped pin to start and immediately found our new tile right on the Start screen.

Internet Explorer has another great new feature called Flip Ahead. Basically, if you're reading an article on a web site that supports it, you can just swipe as if turning the pages of a book to move to the next page instead of searching and tapping next page at the bottom. It's a real time-saver.

This functionality isn't enabled by default (for some reason), so you'll have to change a setting to get it to work. To get started, just swipe in from the right to open the Charms Bar and then tap the Settings charm. From there, tap Internet Options and you'll see the toggle for flip ahead. Tap it to turn it on. That's it. This feature isn't enabled on a whole lot of sites yet, but we managed it just fine on about half of the multi-page articles we read.

Sharing links and articles with friends, another popular web browsing activity, is as easy as bringing up the Charms Bar. For this example, we loaded an article from CNN.com:

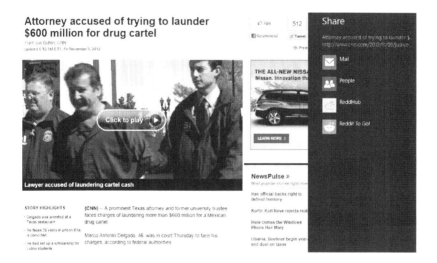

As you can see, tapping 'Share' within the Charms Bar will bring up a list of apps that you can share the article with. We can share via email, to our social networking accounts in the People App, and also to Reddit, a third-party app that we'll discuss a little later.

The best part of this sharing functionality is that it's done within the browser itself – we won't lose our place by exiting Internet Explorer. We tapped 'People' and were greeted with this screen:

Tapping the Facebook icon will allow us to change the social network we'd like to share the article with. Just add a message to the post (if you want to) and tap the send icon. That's it.

Xbox Music – It's an overused phrase, but Xbox Music could very well be Microsoft's killer app. It combines elements of Pandora, Spotify, iTunes, and Grooveshark, forging the music application to end all music applications. Best of all, it's completely free to use on your Surface RT. We'll show you a few tips and shortcuts, but feel free to explore the app on your own – it's truly amazing.

To get started, tap the music tile on the Start screen. Sign in to your Microsoft account (if prompted). After a few seconds, you'll be greeted with the Xbox Music home screen, which will look something like this:

Swiping to the right will reveal all kinds of goodies: featured artists, popular tracks and albums, and even specialized playlists. If you just want to begin listening to an artist right away, tap 'Play an Artist' to bring up a search window. Xbox Music has somewhere around 80 million tracks, so we're pretty sure you'll be able to find what you're looking for, or at least something you'll love. If not, congratulations! You're the pickiest person in the universe. For this example, we decided to search for the popular rock band Modest Mouse:

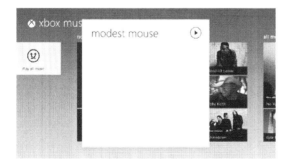

Tapping Modest Mouse from the search field brings up the artist screen. From here, you'll be able to read an artist bio and browse through popular tracks. You can also browse by album:

Tapping 'Play Album' will begin playback. Tapping 'Play Smart DJ' will open a Pandora-like artist radio based on the artist, which also played tracks from bands as disparate as Arcade Fire, The Pixies, and The Shins. Tapping 'Add to My Music' will download the album to your 'My Music' folder, allowing you to play it even if you're offline.

You can also create playlists, purchase tracks, and import your own music. Just tap the corresponding link within the app. The question remains, though: with all of this free stuff, why bother?

Xbox Video – Before you get too excited, Xbox Video isn't free like Xbox Music. This app combines a very functional video player with a storefront that will let you purchase just about any movie or television show you can imagine.

To get started, find the Video tile on your Start screen. You'll be presented with a home screen that looks something like this:

Clicking on the 'Movie' or 'TV' stores will bring you straight to the Video store. From here, you can purchase and download single movies, single television episodes, or even whole seasons.

> *If you haven't already connected your Microsoft account to a payment method, now would be a good time. All you have to do is swipe in from the right to activate the Charms Bar, and then tap Settings. Once you've done that, tap Accounts, and then tap 'Manage Payment Options.' Microsoft is one of the few companies that will accept PayPal as a payment method, which is really handy if you don't want to enter in a bunch of credit card info.*

Of course, you can add your own movies and television shows to the app too. It's a bit of a convoluted process, but will make a lot more sense once you've learned all about the desktop interface. For this example, we'll just go the easy route: USB. Simply copy your movies onto any USB thumb drive, and then insert it into the Surface's USB 2.0 port.

Once you've done that, open the Xbox Video app and swipe up from the bottom. The menu bar will have an icon labeled 'Open File' on the left hand side. Tap that to open the directories your Surface can access. Find your USB drive, and tap on the movie you'd like to watch. For this example, we're going to load the 1999 Kevin Smith movie *Dogma*. As you can see, we put our movies in a folder on the USB drive labeled *Movies*:

Once we've set up HomeGroups and SkyDrive (a little later in this guide), you'll be able to seamlessly connect all of the video content on your home computer(s) to the device. We just don't want to overwhelm you with concepts that we haven't fully explained yet.

Once you've tapped on the movie you'd like to watch, it will automatically begin playing within the Xbox Video app. Tap anywhere on the screen to bring up video options. From there, you can pause, rewind or fast forward, or exit playback by tapping the home icon.

Dogma (1999).avi

That pretty much covers the major pre-installed apps on your Surface RT. Now, let's spend a little time with the Microsoft App Store, and learn how to download some apps of our own.

Downloading Third-Party Apps

We've already shown you a few things you can do with your Surface tablet, but we've only just begun – there are thousands of third party apps waiting for you to download. At the end of this section, we'll recommend some of our favorites, but keep in mind that the App Store is updated on a near-constant basis – what we love today might be tomorrow's old, outdated news.

To get started, go ahead and tap the 'Store' tile on your home screen. You'll be greeted with the Store home screen, which will look more or less like this:

The 'Spotlight' area is usually reserved for the latest and greatest apps that the store has to offer. Swiping right to left will take you to various category lists, including games, social networking, productivity, and health, among others. Just tap a category or a tile to delve deeper. For instance, tapping the 'Top Free' tile will bring up a list of the most popular free apps, while tapping any of the categories will show you both free and paid apps within that category.

To download an app, just tap on it to bring up the app page, then tap install (if it's a free app) or buy (if it's not). Some apps have a third option that will allow you to try a paid app before buying it. This is labeled – appropriately enough – 'Try.'

The app page itself is full of information. You can read a detailed synopsis, alongside user-submitted reviews. This is also where you'll find content ratings, if you care about that kind of thing.

Once you've tapped to install an app, you'll be taken back to the App Store home screen. When the app has finished installing, a notification will appear in the top right-hand corner of the device. It will disappear on its own in a few seconds and will look something like this:

SkyDrive

Microsoft has included 10 GB of SkyDrive cloud storage with every Surface tablet. Users of cloud storage services like Dropbox or iCloud will be familiar with the concept behind Microsoft's SkyDrive, but the company's take on it is a little bit different, especially for the Surface RT.

Basically, SkyDrive is a folder (or group of folders) stored on the Internet, but accessible only to you and your devices. Copying a file from your computer to SkyDrive will make the file available pretty much instantaneously across all of your other SkyDrive-enabled devices.

For example, let's say you've written a document in Word on your PC. You're sitting in the living room, watching television, when you suddenly remember a paragraph or two you've forgotten to include. You can just pull the same file up on your Surface tablet and edit it without having to trudge back to your home office. The changes you make from the living room will automatically be applied to the file on your PC.

To get started, we'll have to download the SkyDrive application to whichever devices you'd like. In Windows 8 or on your Surface tablet, that's as easy as searching for the app in the App Store and downloading it. If you're using another operating system, like OSX, Windows 7, or Windows Vista, it's a little bit more complicated.

To download the application, head over to **www.microsoft.com**. Once there, you'll notice a search bar in the upper right hand corner. Type 'SkyDrive' in the search bar and click search. The first result will be the SkyDrive app. Click again to download it.

Once it's downloaded, click to open the file and install it. Follow the prompts and enter your Microsoft ID and password in the fields. Make sure it's the same ID you use on your Surface. That's all there is to it. You'll now have a folder on your desktop that looks like this:

Copy whatever you like to it: documents, music, videos, etc. Whatever you copy will almost instantly appear within the SkyDrive app on your Surface:

As a special bonus to users of Windows 8, installing SkyDrive will allow you to synchronize the settings of all of your Windows 8 and Windows RT devices. Your tile layout, background, system settings – all of it will match up perfectly if you want it to. Of course, you always have the ability to opt-out.

Now that you've set up the SkyDrive app, you can share the files on your Surface to it. It's as easy as swiping in the charms bar and tapping Share:

Office 2013 RT

One of the major selling points of the Surface, Office 2013 RT is a powerful, full-featured office suite. It's capable of doing pretty much anything you can do with Microsoft Office on your PC. The best part? It's included absolutely free with your Surface. Let's take a quick look at the things you can do with this device.

> *Microsoft, for whatever reason, warns its users that it prohibits using Office RT for "commercial, nonprofit, or revenue-generating activities." So, you know, don't do that.*

To get started, open any of the four Office programs that come with the Surface – Word, Excel, PowerPoint, or OneNote. You can find them on the Start Screen, where the tiles will look like this:

You can also find them in Desktop mode, which we'll discuss a little later. In desktop mode, the Office icons look just like their full-fledged Windows counterparts and are pinned to the bottom of the screen:

Either way, opening these apps will immediately take you into the Desktop mode. A full Office RT tutorial is beyond the scope of this guide, so let's take a more detailed look at the app we think you'll spend the most time in: Word.

Microsoft Word is the world's most popular word processing application on the planet. Using Word, you can create almost any type of document you can think of: short stories, letters, to-do lists, birthday cards – the list is practically endless.

When you open Word 2013 RT for the first time, you'll be greeted with a home screen that looks like this:

You can choose a blank document and start writing right away, or you can choose from dozens of different templates, which are pre-formatted versions of many of the things you might like to create. To save space, these templates aren't stored on the device itself, so tapping on one will pause the action for a moment or two while the template downloads. You'll notice a search bar along the top – use this to find a template that isn't in the list.

Tap to select a blank document or template. This will open the document for editing. For this example, we're using a blank document, but all of this applies to template documents as well. Once you're inside the editing window, you can craft your document in exactly the same way you would on the desktop. The only difference is in the menu.

The menu (or ribbon as it's officially referred to) consists of all the options you have available to you while creating or editing a document. In Office RT, this area is usually touch-optimized. It consists of nine categories and a few icons.

Document1 - Word

FILE   HOME   INSERT   DESIGN   PAGE LAYOUT   REFERENCES   MAILINGS   REVIEW   VIEW

- File is where you'll open new files, save existing ones and exit without saving. This is also where you'll print your documents, assuming you have a printer associated with your Surface. If you have it installed, Word (and all the other Office RT programs) will save your work to SkyDrive by default, making sure you'll have a copy of it wherever you're working.
- Home is where you control the look of your document. Word is a 'what you see is what you get' (WYSIWYG) program, which allows you to change aspects like font size and type and also to change your words into bold, italics and underlines – all while seeing, in real time, what your finished document will look like.
- Insert is the menu that controls all of the elements of your document that are not the main text. From here, you can add pictures, clipart, hyperlinks, charts, or even graphs. This is also where you'll find menus for headers and footers.
- Design is all about the style of your document. Here, you can add stylized titled and paragraphs, giving your document a unique look. You can also control the paragraph spacing from this menu.
- Page layout is where you can adjust settings like margin spacing and indentations and add (or remove) page numbers. You can also split up your text into columns, useful for newspaper or newsletter type documents.
- References will allow you to insert footnotes and endnotes to your text, which is useful for term papers and essays. From here, you can create a uniform, concise bibliography and an index table for your document.

- Mailings is the menu that controls everything related to mailing documents. Here, you can create envelopes, design a template for letters, and manage recipients. For instance, you can create a form letter and a customized envelope for dozens of different people using one document by using what's called a 'mail merge.' It's a neat feature, but explaining further would be well out of the scope of this guide.
- Review comes in handy when you've finished writing your document. This is where you'll check spelling and grammar, but you can also create comments on the text (for later editing) and restrict further editing to protect your document from accidental changes. Since the Surface has a touch screen, this area is also home to an option called 'inking.' This allows you to draw (with your finger) on the document, in much the same way that a teacher would – you can circle things, cross things out, add smiley faces or a grade – the sky's the limit. There are dozens of 'ink' colors to choose from.

In the upper left-hand corner of the screen, you'll notice a few icons:

This is called the quick access toolbar. By default, it will display six items:

- The Window toggle – allows you to resize or close the current window
- The Save button – allows you to save your work

- Undo – allows you to move backwards in your document editing, one step at a time
- Redo – allows you to move forwards in your document editing, one step at a time
- Touch toggle – switches between tablet-optimized menus and keyboard/mouse optimized menus

The touch toggle is actually a really neat feature. All of the menus we just discussed exist in two separate layouts, one of them made especially for touch – with wider areas between options, and bigger fonts. The difference can be subtle, but it's an effective solution. As an example, here is the difference between the touch Home menu and the regular Home menu:

As you can see, the touch version (above) is just a little bit easier to manipulate with your fingers. The options are all the same; just a little easier to touch. The menus for the other Office RT apps function in exactly the same way, albeit with some very different options.

Now that you've got a pretty good grasp of the things your Surface tablet can do, let's dig a little deeper still and discuss a few of the more advanced concepts and settings.

Ready? Let's go!

Part Three: Advanced Tips and Tricks

So far, even though we've learned to do just about everything the average person would need to do with the Surface, your device still has a lot more going on under the hood. As the saying goes, driving a car doesn't make you a mechanic. With that in mind, let's check out some of the functions that will turn you into a Surface master.

The Desktop Interface

In the last section, we briefly visited the desktop interface while using the Office 2013 RT programs. You may have noticed that it looks a lot like the standard desktop version of Windows that you've used for years. The truth is that, aside from the inability to install new programs, that's exactly what it is. Windows RT, which is the underlying operating system that the Surface runs on, is nothing more than a mobile-optimized version of Windows 8. All you have to do to get to the Desktop is tap the tile on the Start screen.

Once you're in desktop mode, you'll notice that there are two additional icons on the bottom taskbar. One is the desktop version of Internet Explorer (more on that in a minute) and the other is the familiar Windows Explorer icon. Tapping here will open an Explorer Window, giving you total access to the Surface, just like with a traditional PC.

From here, you can copy, move, and delete files, open music, video, and office documents, and navigate the directories of any computers on your network.

While all the settings and customization options within the Start screen interface are plenty for some, tinkerers and people more accustomed to traditional Windows might breathe a sigh of relief when they see the familiar Windows control panel, which you can access by simply typing the words 'control panel' into any explorer window's navigation bar:

From here, you can manage all of the Surface's settings – everything from the clock to user accounts.

Feel free to play around, but be forewarned: you can screw things up, just like you can on a desktop or laptop PC, so if you're unfamiliar with something, don't mess with it.

The 'Other' Internet Explorer

Also on the desktop's taskbar, the Internet Explorer icon will open the web browser, but not the same one as on the Surface's Start screen. This version of Internet Explorer has a lot more in common with the desktop version. For starters, the navigation bar is on top, alongside traditional desktop browser tabs.

Basically, this 'extra' version of Internet Explorer is for power users, people who want (or need) to use a full-fledged desktop browser instead of a touch-optimized version. The reasons are many and varied, but as an example, many corporate web sites don't have mobile versions, so using the desktop web browser might be the only way to access it. In most cases, however, the two seem to function in pretty much the same way, and we were shown the same versions of most websites.

Interestingly, this desktop IE interface is also the *only* way to change your home page to something other than the default **www.msn.com**. Changing it on the desktop, however, *will* change it on the Start screen.

To do this (and also access other common settings), go ahead and start up desktop Internet Explorer by tapping its icon on the taskbar. Once you've done this, look for the row of icons near the top right. You'll see an icon representing a house, a star, and a cog. Tap (or click) the cog. Once you've done that, look for the menu item labeled 'Internet Options' near the bottom. Tap (or click) that to bring up the internet options box. The first item you see will be the home page box. Type whatever you'd like your home page to be in that box. Don't worry –you can always change it back by tapping the 'use default' button. Once you've typed in your new home page, make sure to click 'apply' at the bottom. That's it. Your desktop and Start screen versions of Internet Explorer will share the same new home page:

PC Settings and Customization

Earlier, we discussed the Charms Bar and the settings menu within it. However, there is another settings menu within that one: it's called PC Settings, and the vast majority of customization options are located inside.

To get started, swipe in from the right to bring up the Charms Bar, and then tap 'Settings.' Once there, look below the icons to find 'Change PC Settings.' Tapping this will bring up a more advanced all-in-one settings menu, which looks like this:

Let's take a quick look at these more advanced options.

Personalize – Near the beginning of this guide, we were presented with a screen that allowed us to personalize the Start screen. This menu expands on that, allowing you to customize the lock screen, the Start screen, and add an account picture. From here, you can also add items called lock screen apps, which are apps that will show information right on the lock screen. For example, you might want to see a list of recent emails at a glance, without having to open the device and navigate to the mail app.

To do this, just navigate to 'lock screen apps' near the bottom of the 'Personalize' menu. Tap any of the 7 plus symbols to add an app to the lock screen. All of the apps that support this feature will pop up. Find the app you'd like to add and tap it. That's it.

The Start screen personalization options are color coded to make sure that your menus and backgrounds won't clash. Just drag your finger up and down the color bar until you find something you like – the setting updates in real time, so you can get an idea of how it will look before leaving the menu.

Users – This menu will allow you to change your account details—this is where you'll go if you ever need to change your password. This is also where you'll add new users to the device, if you choose to. The Surface, unlike most tablets, supports multiple users, each with their own unique Start screen and file system. In fact, adding a new user will take you through the setup process that we went through at the beginning of this guide.

From here, you can also set up what Microsoft calls a 'Picture Password.' It's a pretty neat way to add some security to your Surface. After setting this up, every time you turn on the Surface, you'll be greeted with a picture that you tap and/or draw on. These custom, invisible actions serve as your password. To get started, just tap 'Create a Picture Password.' You'll be prompted for your account password, so enter that before proceeding. After that, choose a picture and follow the three-step drawing/tapping process, repeat it to make sure you've got it down, and tap 'accept.' That's it.

Notifications- This menu exists to toggle on screen notifications on or off. You can do this for each individual app or for every app you've installed. This is also where you turn off notification sounds.

Search – This controls the behavior of the search function within the Charms bar. You can choose which apps to search, and in what order. This is also where you'll delete the search history if desired. Microsoft saves your search history to help speed up your future searches.

Share – Just like Search, this menu controls the sharing function on the Charms Bar. From here, you can toggle the apps you use to share on or off, and also control the list of 'most shared' items that populates the share charm after using it a few times.

General – Probably the most important setting menu, this area has options for the onscreen keyboard (things like auto-correction and typing sounds), and it also has settings for auto-brightness, languages, date and time, app-switching, and –most importantly – it contains the 'reset' menu. You have two options when it comes to resetting/restoring your device: you can wipe the slate clean and start over from scratch by tapping 'Remove Everything and Reinstall Windows', or you can do what's referred to as a refresh by tapping 'Refresh your PC without Affecting Your Files.' This will reinstall the Windows files but keep your settings and personal files intact. If your Surface seems sluggish—or crashes—this is the way to go.

Privacy – This menu contains a couple of toggles relating to the information you allow Microsoft or third-party apps to collect. Microsoft will never sell your information, or misuse it in any way, but they still give you the option, just to be on the safe side.

Devices –This menu brings up a list of devices you've connected to your Surface – everything from smartphones to printers to computers on your network will be displayed here. If you want to permanently disconnect a device from your Surface, just tap the minus symbol next to the device. If you want to add a device that the Surface hasn't automatically recognized, just tap the plus symbol and follow the prompts.

Wireless –This menu toggles airplane mode on and off, and also controls whether the built in Bluetooth is discoverable or not. You can shut down all wireless communication from here.

Ease of Access- This menu controls settings for the visual or hearing impaired. From here, you can turn up the contrast, making it a little easier to see things, and also turn on the 'Narrator' function, which will make your Surface 'talk' you through the on-screen action. You can also increase the thickness of the onscreen cursor from here, if you're having trouble seeing it at its default size.

Sync Your Settings –if you have a Windows 8 PC, this is where you'll control what aspects of it are synced up with your Surface. From here, you can duplicate your PC's Start screen, settings, sign-in information, and web browser settings.

HomeGroup – If you have other Windows PCs on a HomeGroup (which we'll discuss in the next section), this is where you'll join it. Windows RT won't let you share the Surface's content with a PC, but you can share all of the videos, music, and other files on your desktop or laptop with the Surface.

Windows Update –Tapping here will search Microsoft's servers for any updates to your device. They are updated on a near-constant basis, so check here often for updates that will no doubt offer speed improvements, security fixes, and new features.

Setting up a HomeGroup

Networking your home computers and connecting them with all of your other devices used to be a gargantuan task that required dozens of wires and a whole lot of patience. Since the release of Windows Vista back in 2006, Microsoft has aimed to simplify the process of sharing content across a home network. The resulting solution, called HomeGroup, is easy to set up, and even easier to work with. It's the quickest, most stable way to get all of your PCs content to your Surface tablet.

To get started, head to your desktop or laptop PC. Click the Start menu and type 'HomeGroup' into the search field at the bottom. The first result will be labeled 'HomeGroup.' Click it to begin setting up your HomeGroup.

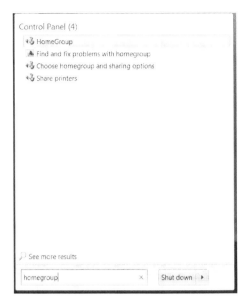

Once you've done that, you'll be presented with the HomeGroup setup screen. Depending on your Windows version, it will look something like this:

Share with other home computers

There is currently no homegroup on the network.

With a homegroup, you can share files and printers with other computers running Windows 7. You can also stream media to devices. The homegroup is protected with a password, and you'll always be able to choose what you share with the group.

Tell me more about homegroups

Change advanced sharing settings...

Start the HomeGroup troubleshooter

Create a homegroup   Cancel

All you have to do from here is click the button that says 'Create a HomeGroup.' Once that's done, you'll be presented with a screen asking you what files and/or libraries you'd like to share with the HomeGroup:

Share with other home computers

Your computer can share files and printers with other computers running Windows 7, and you can stream media to devices using a homegroup. The homegroup is protected with a password, and you'll always be able to choose what you share with the group.

Tell me more about homegroups

Select what you want to share:

☑ Pictures   ☐ Documents

☑ Music   ☑ Printers

☑ Videos

[Next] [Cancel]

Check whichever boxes you want to and click 'Next.' The next screen will show your HomeGroup password. You'll need this to connect your other devices to the HomeGroup, so write it down.

Use this password to add other computers to your homegroup

Before you can access files and printers located on other computers, add those computers to your homegroup. You'll need the following password:

Write down this password:

EA83BT8J85

Print password and instructions

If you ever forget your homegroup password, you can view or change it by opening HomeGroup in Control Panel.

How can other computers join my homegroup?

That's it. Once you've connected your Surface to the HomeGroup (from the PC Settings menu), it should automatically recognize all of your files and allow you to access them in the appropriate places, like Xbox Video, Xbox Music, and Office RT.

Xbox Games and Xbox SmartGlass

Microsoft has integrated their other hardware platform, the Xbox 360, with the Surface in all kinds of ways. If you happen to own the video game console, Xbox Games and Xbox SmartGlass are two pretty amazing tools.

Xbox Games is half store, half social networking app. If you've signed into your Surface with the same Microsoft account as your Xbox 360 (if you haven't, you really should), opening this built-in app will log you in with your Gamer Tag (your Xbox nickname, for those who don't know) and allow you to customize your avatar, read messages from friends, and view and share game achievements with people all over the world. You can also browse game titles for the Xbox, Windows, and the Surface tablet. Purchasing a game for the Xbox from within this app will automatically send it to the device.

The real magic, however, is Xbox SmartGlass. Touted as a second screen for your Xbox 360, this app is all that and more. You'll have to download it from the App Store to get started, but once you do, everything will connect seamlessly. Turn on your Xbox 360 and tap the Xbox SmartGlass tile on your Surface. Once you've done that, you'll be greeted with this screen:

Within a few seconds, your Surface will connect, and it will look – for all intents and purposes – exactly like the screen on your Xbox 360. Once you're connected, you can control virtually every aspect of the Xbox 360 right from your Surface tablet.

For example, we tapped the 'Recently Played' button and were presented with a list of games and apps we recently opened on the Xbox. With one tap, we opened the 'about' screen for the popular Xbox game 'Skate':

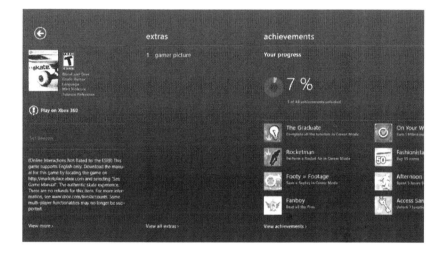

From here, we were able to view our progress in the game, find more information about the title, access the picture of our in-game character, and —with one tap— begin playing the game.

The functionality works great, especially for video. Normally, we'd have to fuss around with an Xbox 360 controller to interact with video streaming apps like Netflix, but with the Surface in hand, we were able to just tap the Netflix program, open it, navigate the menu system, open an episode of the popular TV show *Parks and Recreation*, and then read about the episode – all on the Surface itself using the remote feature, which mimics the Xbox controller's functionality perfectly:

If you have an Xbox 360, we highly recommend this app. The best part? It's completely free to use.

Must-Have Apps

Aside from the many great apps that come pre-installed with your Surface tablet, there are dozens of great applications on the App Store to download and try. Here are a few of the best ones we've come across so far, organized by category.

Social – While the Surface tablet comes with two great social networking apps –People and Messaging, there are still some great applications to download:

Skype (free) – Skype is the best video chat application for any device and the specially optimized version for the Surface tablet is no exception. Since this app exists for pretty much every platform imaginable (iOS, Android, Windows, and Mac), it's super-easy to keep up-to-date with all of your friends and loved ones. Just install and choose a username, if you don't already have one. Skype will even automatically search through your People and Messaging apps to find contacts that are already using the service.

IM+ (free) - If the Messaging app isn't quite enough for you, IM+ will definitely fulfill your requirements. Literally every single messaging platform is included here, allowing you to connect to services like Google Chat, Yahoo! Messenger, AOL Instant Messenger, ICQ, and about a dozen more. IM+ will also connect to Skype, but without support for video.

<u>Reddit to Go! (free)</u> – Reddit is the world's largest social news site. Home to millions of news junkies and witty commentators, you're sure to find a home in one of the thousands of "Sub-Reddits" about almost any topic you can imagine. There are over a dozen Reddit apps in the Microsoft App Store, but this one is the best by a clear mile. Its multi pane interface is somehow an improvement over Reddit.com

Video – While Xbox Video is a perfectly good solution for watching the movies you already own, purchasing and streaming movies can really put a strain on your wallet. Luckily, there are a couple of great video streaming apps that you may want to pick up.

<u>Netflix (free trial, then $9.99 monthly)</u> – Netflix is the king of Internet video streaming. With an enormous catalog of award-winning films and television shows, there's always something to watch. While the Netflix application exists on a variety of platforms, the Surface tablet version is among the fastest and most intuitive we've tried. If you've never used the service before, they'll even let you try it for 30 days before charging you.

<u>Hulu Plus (free trial, then $9.99 monthly)</u> – The main competitor to Netflix, Hulu Plus doesn't have *quite* the level of content of its chief rival, but where it really shines is in episodes of currently airing television shows. Most of the major networks release their shows for streaming on Hulu Plus the day after they've aired, which can be really great for cord-cutters and super-busy people. Sadly, their free trial only lasts 14 days, but the desktop browser version (Hulu without the 'plus') is completely free, with a slightly more limited selection.

Music and Audio – We've already discussed the ridiculously awesome (and free!) Xbox Music streaming service, but there are a couple missing features: FM radio and podcasts. These apps are sure to be music to your ears.

> SlapDash Podcasts (free) – If you don't listen to podcasts, you're missing out. From news, technology, and history to comedy (and everything in between), podcasts are long-form shows about any topic you can imagine. It's sort of like talk radio, but interesting – and better sound quality. SlapDash lets you subscribe to any podcasts on the Internet, then stores them in the cloud, streaming them to you on demand. You can also download podcasts and listen to them right in the app, just in case you're ever without a Wi-Fi signal.

> IHeartRadio (free) – This radio app gives you real-time access to over 1,500 radio stations across the world, and serves up specialty stations like the all-punk CBGB Radio. If that's not enough, you can also create customized, commercial-free radio stations based on the artists you love.

News and Productivity – The built-in news app does a great job of keeping you informed, but there are dozens of news readers and apps for information junkies. Here are two of our favorites.

News Bento (free) – This app is a lot like the built-in news reader: it's intuitive, easy to customize, and very, very elegant looking. Where News Bento really shines, though, is in its ability to integrate with Google Reader, the best way to truly customize your news that we know of.

Wikipedia (free) – If you've been living on Mars for the last several years, you might not already know about Wikipedia. For the uninitiated, Wikipedia is a user-generated digital encyclopedia that has information about any topic you can possibly imagine. We like to tap random and drift from article to article for hours, learning about everything from Mexican haberdashery to equine mating habits. The Windows RT interface is fast and simple –which is exactly what Wikipedia is supposed to be.

Games – The Surface tablet was conceived with productivity in mind. While that's all well and good, if you're like us, you'll spend a significant amount of time playing games with this device. New games are being released for the Surface all the time, but we've chosen two favorites that have some serious, addictive staying power.

Angry Birds: Star Wars ($4.99) – If you've ever used a mobile device, chances are you played the original Angry Birds on it. This follow-up to the most popular video game of all time pits the loveable birds against the Empire (of pigs). Even if you're not a fan of the Star Wars movies, you *will* become addicted to this game, we pretty much guarantee it.

Pinball FX 2 (free, additional content starts at $1.99) –
Another Microsoft-created app, this old-school pinball
machine takes full advantage of the Surface's taller-than-
average portrait mode to faithfully recreate the look and feel
of classic pinball. You can even battle with your friends with
the two-player 'hotseat' mode.

Conclusion

Now that we've taken you through some of the amazing things you can do with your Surface tablet, you're ready to teach a community college extension class on this thing. We're sure that you're going to get years of enjoyment out of this powerful and unique device, finding new, amazing uses for it – things we haven't even thought of yet. We sincerely hope that you enjoyed this guide half as much as we enjoyed writing it.

Happy Surfacing!